THE SECRET LETTERS PROJECT

JULIET MADISON

This publication is designed to provide accurate and authoritative information
in regard to the subject matter covered. It is sold with the understanding
that the publisher is not engaged in rendering legal, accounting, or other
professional service. If legal advice or other expert assistance is required,
the services of a competent professional person should be sought.—*From a
Declaration of Principles Jointly Adopted by a Committee of the American Bar
Association and a Committee of Publishers and Associations*

Published by Sourcebooks, Inc.
P.O. Box 4410, Naperville, Illinois 60567-4410
(630) 961-3900
Fax: (630) 961-2168
www.sourcebooks.com

Library of Congress Cataloging-in-Publication data
is on file with the publisher.

Printed and bound in China.
LEO 10 9 8 7 6 5 4 3 2 1

BENEFITS OF
LETTER WRITING

Real-life testimonials from people who have used
secret letters to create positive impacts:

"They have been amazingly healing."

–Ruth

"I did one after my relationship breakup. It was just pages
of what I was feeling, and it was a good exercise to let
go of past beliefs and behaviors and choices, which then
helped attract the beautiful, kind man I'm with now."

–Fleur

"I wrote Dear Diary entries, like letters to God, and the answers to my questions always came, quicker than I expected! Organizing thoughts is empowering, no matter where we're at in life. Had I not taken the time to study my psychological defects (through writing), I may never have cleaned up my act and overcome my drug addiction."

—Tristan

"I've done hundreds. Ritual is so important to me with each one; I burn them or place them in the ocean. It helps me and is never intended for anyone else to see."

—Julia

"I've written to my parents, my siblings, my ex, and my inner child. I stuff it in an envelope, write an address or c/o the Universe, then burn it."

—Jodie

"Mine always started with anger. Then once I'd released all of that, it was forgiveness of the person and myself."

—Tracey

"What I found was that I was the instigator of attracting what I didn't like about another person or what hurt me, purely from beliefs I had about myself. Everything came back to ME, not in a self-abusive way, but in an empowering way, because, God, if I created this, what could I create if I let those beliefs go? So I did."

—Fleur

"Several years ago, I was going through a really rough patch. So I got the idea of writing a letter to an imaginary friend. I gave the friend my middle name (Gisela) and started each letter with 'Dear Gisela' as if I were writing to a real person. I just wrote whatever came to my mind. It was cathartic, letting it all out, putting it into words, and knowing that I wouldn't be judged. I carefully read each letter once it was finished, and that helped clear my thoughts.

Then, I'd tear it into small shreds and throw it away, which brought relief."

—Devika

"Letter writing has helped me to set my intentions and put into practice visualization for the future. I believe setting intentions for the future is a wonderful way of creating the life you want—what you put out into the universe is what comes back. Writing letters has opened my mind to the divine guidance that I know flows inside me, and when I take the time to quiet myself and write with all that intention, something very special happens and a knowing builds within that is stronger than just the thought."

—Shannon

LETTER LIST

To Jay.

*It's no secret that you're the best thing
that ever happened to me.*

HOW TO USE THIS BOOK

....

Dear Reader,

It is with great pleasure that I write to you today, as I prepare to share with you the tools and tips for writing healing and empowering letters like those that have helped me in my own life.

When I go through a difficult time, I often put pen to paper and pour out what is inside my heart, making sense of the emotions. Knowing that I can express myself through a letter at any time brings great comfort, and so it has become an important part of my life in helping me work through things and keeping focused on turning challenges into positive learning experiences. It has also helped me enhance positive situations by giving me an outlet to express gratitude and excitement for what is happening and what is to come.

You may be going through something challenging in your

life right now. You may have emotions swirling up inside that you are struggling to make sense of, making you wonder how to express them or making you confused about how to move forward. I understand. I've been there. And I can help.

Letter writing was once one of the most common forms of communication, before the technology that we know today existed. Whether used as a simple means of communication and planning, a way to express feelings and yearnings for someone, or a way to share details about your life or experiences with a loved one far away, letter writing was an important part of life in historical times. With modern technology and the Internet having changed communication from slow and thoughtful to instant and brief, many people have forgotten about the simple act of writing a letter and how it can be of immense value to both the writer and the recipient. In addition, many people are unaware of how writing a secret letter, a letter just for themselves, can be a powerful tool to deal with challenging circumstances or to simply generate excitement for life and anticipation for the future.

Some people write random musings in journals to release thoughts and emotions; some express themselves through mindful coloring and art therapy; some write long lists and detailed goals and plans; others talk to friends or therapists; and some, sadly, keep everything bottled up inside. Writing secret letters is a way for all kinds of people to improve their emotional health and break free of blockages holding them back.

With letters, you can be as open or as secretive as you like. Letter writing can be your private, personal outlet or something you discuss and share with others. It is up to you how you make use of this tool. And this book will show you exactly how to write a letter, from deciding what type of letter to write, to thinking of what to write and creating a meaningful ritual to acknowledge or release your letter and help you move forward.

Would you like to deal better with grief? Would you like some closure about a problem or issue that is weighing on your mind? Would you like to attract something or someone special into your life? These are just some of the reasons to write a secret letter.

Have a look through the Letter List. Which type of letter jumps out at you? Which letter would be most helpful for you right now? Start with that. Read the instructions, the examples (some of which are real letters from contributors, and some of which were created specifically for this book), and then use the template to craft your letter from beginning to end. You may choose to write on beautiful stationery, plain paper, within this journal, or in another meaningful book or diary—whatever feels right to you.

As you write, tune into your emotions and innermost thoughts and beliefs. Don't hold back. It's okay if your letter starts with negative emotion. Allow yourself to go through the process, and aim to include something positive with each letter. If the issue you are writing about is particularly stressful, you may wish to have a friend or therapist help you. If writing by hand is difficult, you may type it up or have a trusted friend write it for you as you speak. Don't worry about grammar or spelling. It's okay if you cross parts out or make mistakes. What matters is the emotion behind the words and the effort to make something positive out of the experience.

When you've completed your letter, do what feels right with it. In some cases, you may actually give it to a recipient, but only do this if it will enhance the person's well-being or assist a positive outcome. If it won't, then use the experience as a way to help yourself instead. You may burn the letter or rip it up and discard it—remember, the power is in the process, not in the actual physical letter. Unless the paper used has synthetic materials, like a plastic coating or embellishments, you may place it in the ocean or a lake, or bury it. You could hide it away, place it with a meaningful memento, put it behind a special photo in a frame, paint over it to create a meaningful and secret piece of art, place it in a special "letter box," send it in the mail to yourself, or anything that allows you to release it in a positive way. If you like, you can also do rituals while writing and/or before releasing the letter, such as lighting candles, listening to music, placing crystals on it, blessing it, kissing it, hugging it, folding it up tightly, decorating it, and putting it in an envelope. Or if you'd prefer to just write the letter within this journal and leave it at that, that's perfectly fine as well.

As you start to include therapeutic letter writing as part

of your life, you may find your overall communication skills improve. The more you get used to expressing yourself, the easier it gets. You may wish to incorporate a letter writing ritual into your routine, for example, on 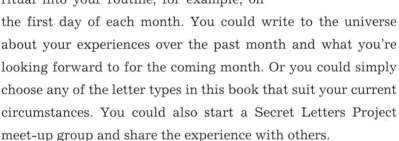 the first day of each month. You could write to the universe about your experiences over the past month and what you're looking forward to for the coming month. Or you could simply choose any of the letter types in this book that suit your current circumstances. You could also start a Secret Letters Project meet-up group and share the experience with others.

Remember, writing secret letters is a powerful way to not only aid in emotional healing, but to also enhance your well-being and create a more meaningful, positive life.

I would love to hear how your secret letter writing goes. Write to me and let me know.

Love,

Juliet xo

PS If you would like to share any of your secret letters with other secret letter writers or discuss your experiences, follow the link at julietmadison.com for the Secret Letters Project Facebook group, or submit via the website, and your letter may be shared anonymously on your behalf.

LETTER #1

DEAR STRANGER

....

Perform a random and anonymous act of kindness
by writing an inspiring letter to a stranger.

WHY WRITE TO A STRANGER?

You may have heard of random acts of kindness, whereby people
leave gifts or surprises for strangers in public or perform a kind
deed, such as paying for the coffee for the person behind you in
line. Writing an anonymous letter is one such gift you can give. It
feels good, it's exciting, and you never know—it may just make
someone's day or even change their life. Never underestimate the
power of inspiring words. Giving kindness enriches the heart and

soul, and what you give out in life you get in return. The key with this is to not have any idea who is going to get your letter and not try to find out. The joy is in not knowing, wondering what their face looks like when they read your letter, and knowing that, most likely, your gift was gratefully received.

WHAT TO DO WITH THE LETTER:

Place your letter in an envelope. You may wish to write on the envelope "Dear You" or "Dear Stranger" or "For Whoever Finds This." You can either plan ahead where to leave it or wander around and allow your intuition to guide you to the right place.

Here are some ideas:

In a public park (weather permitting, or placed in a plastic bag)

In a doctor's waiting room

At the gym

In a library on a shelf or inside a book

At a bookstore

Under the windshield wiper of someone's car

In a shopping cart

In a pay phone booth

At an automatic teller machine

In a stranger's mailbox

In an elevator

HOW TO WRITE IT:

Think of a tough day you've had and what would have made you feel better. What words, phrases, or positive sayings come to mind? Imagine the person receiving your letter is having a bad day, or perhaps they are having a good day, and when they receive your letter, they are going to feel even better. Write about positive things you have learned in life, supportive words of encouragement, or a reminder that each and every person is special and a valuable part of life. You may even simply write something like "Dear Stranger, I hope you have an amazing day!" The letter can be as long or short as you wish. As you write, imagine the recipient with a big smile on their face as they read your words.

You may choose to leave it unsigned, write your first name, or write something like "from one stranger to another," "from anonymous," "from me," or "from a friend."

EXAMPLES:

Dear Stranger,

You might be wondering what this is all about. Why would someone leave an anonymous letter for someone else to find? The reason is simple. There is a lot of negativity in the world, but I am choosing to spread joy and kindness. I would like to wish you an amazing day, and I hope all your dreams come true. Always believe in yourself, never give up, and keep smiling.

Love,
your anonymous friend

To the person who finds this...

If you are having a bad day, stop, breathe, and remember the big picture. You are alive. You are breathing. You have eyes that can see and read this letter. You have a lot to be thankful for. Sometimes life is hard, but sometimes it is beautiful. Focus on the beautiful parts, and keep positive.

If you are not having a bad day, then that's great! Keep doing what you're doing, and maybe you'd like to leave this letter for someone else to find. Pay it forward.

Either way, remember that you are a special person with unique gifts that are of value to the world. Keep being you.

BEFORE YOU WRITE YOUR LETTER...

Complete the following sentences so you and your recipient both get the most out of the experience:

1. I would like to write a letter to a stranger because...

    ....
    ....
    ....

2. After writing this letter, I would like to feel...

    ....
    ....
    ....

3. After reading this letter, I would like the recipient to feel...

    ....
    ....
    ....

4. Ideas on places I could leave this letter are...

    ....
    ....
    ....

TEMPLATE AND GUIDE TO WRITE YOUR OWN:

1. Dear (stranger, you, amazing person, fellow human, friend):

2. Decide on your intention for the recipient. What would you like them to feel or come away with after reading your letter (e.g., to put a smile on their face, to make them laugh, to lift their spirits, to remind them of their value)?

3. Think of some key words that could resonate with your intention, e.g., important, valuable, special, kindness, gifts, laughter, smile, hope, dreams. Then, craft your letter around these key words, getting your intent across through empowering and uplifting words.

4. Consider drawing a smiley face, a cartoon, a flower, a heart, or any other positive symbol to add a special touch.

5. Seal it in an envelope and write on the envelope so the person who finds it knows they can open it.

6. Decide where to leave the letter. Place it somewhere and then leave with a smile, knowing that your work is done.

....
....
....
....
....
....
....
....
....
....
....
....
....
....
....
....
....
....
....
....
....
....
....
....
....
....
....

DEAR LOVED ONE

Move through the grieving process by writing
a letter to your deceased loved one.

WHY WRITE TO A DECEASED LOVED ONE?

Sometimes when a person dies, we wish we could speak to them again, tell them things we never got to say to them, and discuss our lives. Whether you believe in the afterlife or not, writing a letter to a deceased loved one can help you release built-up emotions, express things that have yet to be expressed, or simply help you feel close to them. Anything and everything you wish to say to them can be said, so don't hold back. If you had a great relationship with your loved one, tell them everything you loved about them and how they impacted your life. If you had a difficult relationship, release any disappointments and express yourself, but also think of how those challenges helped you grow and learn more about life, people, and yourself.

This type of letter can be great for emotional expression, providing closure, giving gratitude, reminiscing, and acknowledging the value of a person's life.

WHAT TO DO WITH THE LETTER:

You may keep the letter, show it to friends and family, or discard the letter to give yourself closure.

Here are some ideas:

Place it behind a photo of your loved one in a frame
Put it with one of your loved one's belongings
Place it in an envelope on a memory shelf
Take it to their grave and read it aloud, then place it on the grave
Let it get washed away in the ocean
Burn it as a ceremonial release to the universe

HOW TO WRITE IT:

Consider the impact this person had on your life. What memories did you share? What did you learn from them? What was something they always used to say or do? What made them unique? Remember them being in your life and write what comes to mind. You may like to play your loved one's favorite music as you write, burn a candle or use an essential oil they would have liked the smell of, spray their favorite perfume or cologne, or sit in their favorite chair or favorite coffee shop.

Honor their uniqueness and the gifts they brought to the world and your life, and end the letter with why you will never forget them.

EXAMPLES:

Dear Grandma,

You were always there for me, and I'm grateful for that. I'll never forget you. I love how you used to give me chocolate and sweets when my parents weren't looking!

You were both gentle in nature and fierce in your love. You would have done anything for your family. I always felt fully supported by you. Whether it was just a chat, a hug, some words of wisdom, or most importantly, chocolate and sweets, you always offered some kind of help. One thing I'll never forget that you always used to tell me was, "Things always seem better in the morning." You were right. There is not much a good sleep can't fix.

I loved your enthusiasm for life, your can-do attitude, and your kind heart. You taught me how to stay positive, how to keep moving forward, and how to focus on what is most important in life.

Thank you for being there, for being you, and for allowing me to be me.

Love forever,
Your favorite grandchild :)

Dear Lucy,

I know we didn't always see eye to eye, but I realize now that despite our differences, you were loyal, both to me and our family. As sisters, I always wished we could have been closer, done things that other sisters did, had a stronger bond, but we were so different. And that's okay, because in hindsight, it has taught me about unconditional love and acceptance.

I want to forgive you for the times that I felt you hurt me, and I want to ask you to forgive me for the times you felt I hurt you. I know we were both just doing what we thought was right for ourselves.

Now that you're gone, I don't want to harbor any resentment. I only want to remember your loyalty, your strong will, and your dedication to what you believed in. I am proud of you for that and glad you were my sister.

Helen

BEFORE YOU WRITE YOUR LETTER...

Complete the following sentences:

1. I would like to write a letter to my loved one in spirit because...

....

....

....

2. After writing this letter, I would like to feel...

....

....

....

3. I imagine if my loved one could read this letter, they would feel...

....

....

....

4. Some ideas on ways I could acknowledge, store, or release this letter are...

....

....

....

5. Positive key words and traits that come to mind when I think of my loved one are...

....

....

....

TEMPLATE AND GUIDE TO WRITE YOUR OWN:

1. Dear (loved one's name)...

2. Think of your earliest memory of them. Describe it.

3. What was their personality like? Acknowledge their unique traits and individuality.

4. Recall something they often did or said and write about it.

5. What did you love most about them?

6. What did you learn from them?

7. What are some of your most memorable experiences, funniest moments, or most meaningful moments with them?

8. Tell them what their life brought to the world and your life. Give gratitude.

9. If you could say one thing to them now, what would it be?

10. Place the letter in an envelope if you wish, or simply fold it, and release it by whichever method feels right to you.

....
....
....
....
....
....
....
....
....
....
....
....
....
....
....
....
....
....
....
....
....
....
....
....
....
....

....
....
....
....
....
....
....
....
....
....
....
....
....
....
....
....
....
....
....
....
....
....
....
....
....
....
....
....

LETTER #3

DEAR SOUL MATE

....

Consciously connect with the heart and soul
of the future partner you're hoping to find.

WHY WRITE TO YOUR SOUL MATE
OR FUTURE PARTNER?

If you haven't yet met or united with the special person you'd
like to spend your life with, but you believe they are out there
somewhere, why not write them a letter? It could be fun to show
them one day, or you may wish to keep it hidden. The power of
this type of letter is it harnesses the law of attraction, bringing
into your life those elements you put your focus on and your

heart and soul into. A soul mate letter is a great way to discover what you would like in a partner and to show trust and belief in the universe that they are out there and that you can find them. It is also a way to find out what you really want to give and receive in a relationship and how a relationship can become part of your life.

WHAT TO DO WITH THE LETTER:

This is a letter you may wish to keep for the future, in case you wish to show it to your soul mate/partner when you unite with them. However, you can still release it symbolically in water or by burning if you wish.

If you're going to keep it, you could store it in a special decorative box, in an envelope under your pillow, on your bedside table on the side they would sleep on, or in a drawer. You may even wish to stick it up on a wall, corkboard, or vision board.

HOW TO WRITE IT:

Take a few moments to close your eyes and breathe deeply. Visualize what your life would be like with your soul mate in it. What are you doing, saying, talking about? What qualities do they have? Get a clear picture of the type of person they are and the types of things you will do together. Focus on the feelings and how your life and theirs will be enhanced by your relationship.

Then write to them and tell them how you feel and why you love having them in your life, or tell them what you are looking forward to when you finally meet. You can write it in present tense, as though they are in your life already, or write it about the future, as a way of showing your anticipation around meeting them. Have fun with it and let your personality and true nature shine through.

EXAMPLES:

*This example is from the novel *April's Glow* by Juliet Madison, published in April 2016 by Escape Publishing:

Dear Soul Mate,

I already love you. Even though we're not yet together, and I don't know who you are or whether we've met or are yet to meet, I already feel a deep love and connection with you. I woke this morning with a strong urge to write to you, my mystery woman, my future best friend, lover, soul mate.

If you walked into my life right now, I would want you, but I wouldn't be ready. I will be one day, but not yet. There are things I need to take care of, things I need to resolve. I need to get my life back on track and be the man you would want to have in your life. That is keeping me going, knowing that you are out there somewhere in this vast universe, and it is up to me to be the best man I can be. Not only for you, but for me.

Maybe you're on a journey too, finding your way in the world, or overcoming personal trauma or challenges. If you are, I know you'll come out on top. I can already tell that you're a strong, inspiring woman. Somehow, I have this sense of you, like we're already bonded by our future, though it hasn't happened yet. I feel a kind of promise, a knowing, that you are on your way to me and I am on my way to you. It could be in a year, or it could be in five years. Who knows? But I trust that perfect timing will be on our side.

I love knowing that as my heart beats, so too does yours. As my lungs breathe oxygen, so do yours. Right this minute. I exist. You exist. And one day we will exist together. I will place my hand on your heart and feel your heart beating. I will be close to you, breathe the same air you are breathing, feel your breath on my skin. You will no longer be a thought, a hope, a dream, but my reality.

If I am brave enough to show you this letter, it means I've looked into your eyes and realized that you're the woman I've written this letter to. It will be the most magical moment of my life, knowing that you're her. And I'll never take you, or us, for granted. You're so important to me. Even now, not knowing what you look like, what your favorite food is, or how you sound when you laugh, you're important. All I know now is your essence, the core of who you are. I can feel that deep in my heart, beating along with my own.

My beautiful partner, always remember this:
I love you.
I loved you before I loved you.
I loved you before we were us.

Thank you for coming into my life, for taking a chance on me, for accepting me. Let's make every moment count.

Love,
Zac

BEFORE YOU WRITE YOUR LETTER...

Complete the following sentences:

1.   I would like to write a letter to my soul mate because...

   ....
   ....
   ....

2.   After writing this letter, I would like to feel...

   ....
   ....
   ....

3.   If my soul mate reads this letter, I would like them to feel...

   ....
   ....
   ....

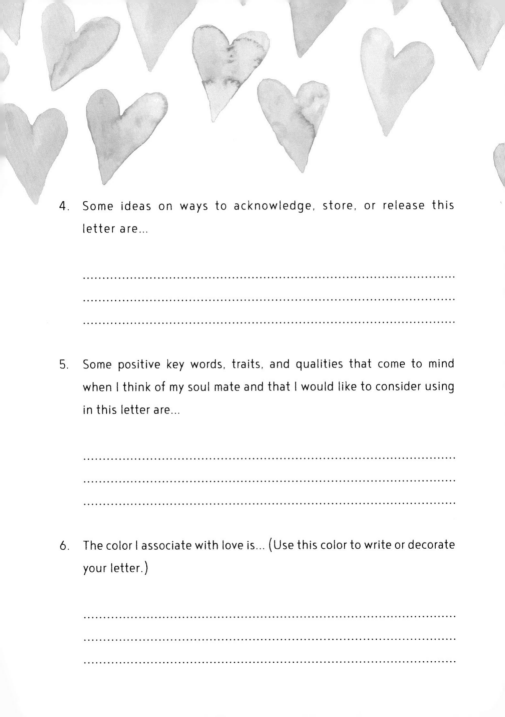

4. Some ideas on ways to acknowledge, store, or release this letter are...

....
....
....

5. Some positive key words, traits, and qualities that come to mind when I think of my soul mate and that I would like to consider using in this letter are...

....
....
....

6. The color I associate with love is... (Use this color to write or decorate your letter.)

....
....
....

TEMPLATE AND GUIDE TO WRITE YOUR OWN:

1. Dear Soul Mate/Lover/Partner/Husband/Wife or whichever term you prefer.

2. Tell them how much you are looking forward to meeting them and that you are open and trusting about who, when, and how things will unfold.

3. Tell them about your life now, what you love about it, and what you will love even more about it when they are part of it.

4. Explain what you love about them, the type of person you think they'll be, the quirks they may have, the things they might say or do, and the gifts they may bring to your life.

5. Talk about the things you'll do together, where you might live, the places you'll travel, and whether you'll have kids and who they'll take after the most.

6. Tell them that even though you haven't met yet (as far as you know), you already love them and you love that they are out in the world somewhere, living their life and preparing to meet you one day.

7. You might also like to think of some way of knowing they are the right one for you, something they may say to you or do, or a unique common interest you have, and tell them that you'll know them when that particular thing happens or comes up.

8. Sign the letter with your name or a nickname you may like them to call you.

9. Decide on a meaningful way to store or release the letter, and trust that if you believe this person is out there, they will arrive when the timing is right for both of you.

....
....
....
....
....
....
....
....
....
....
....
....
....
....
....
....
....
....
....
....
....
....
....
....
....
....
....
....

LETTER #4

DEAR ME

....

Write an empowering letter to yourself
as an act of self-love and acceptance.

WHY WRITE TO YOURSELF?

Why not? It might feel silly, but the words you say to yourself, whether spoken or written, can have a profound effect on your thoughts, beliefs, and experiences. Writing to yourself is a powerful way of rewiring your brain with positive thoughts that will better serve you in life and help you be more comfortable in your own skin. It is also an act of self-love. Self-love and self-acceptance are the first steps to experiencing good health, happiness, and love in your life. Everything starts with the self, even the people and experiences in your life. By consciously working on your own thoughts and beliefs, you are consciously creating your life experience.

Letter writing to the self is also a way to discover and understand yourself more fully, which is valuable for emotional health and helps you understand others.

WHAT TO DO WITH THE LETTER:

For this type of letter, you may wish to keep a special journal or memento box for letters to yourself, so you can reread them. Writing to yourself regularly is a bit like journaling or keeping a diary, except you are writing directly to yourself as opposed to some other unseen entity.

If you have something particularly important to tell or remind yourself, you may even wish to drop it in the mail, so you officially receive it.

HOW TO WRITE IT:

Tell yourself what you know and like about yourself, your positive attributes, challenges you have overcome, things you have learned, and things you are looking forward to learning, embracing, or experiencing. Treat yourself with respect and love, as you would a friend.

Another option is to complete a thirty-day self-love challenge by writing a brief sentence or two about yourself every night for thirty days. The sentences are like mini-letters that affirm your value and worthiness, and by writing consistently for thirty days, you are imprinting a new positive self-talk habit into your mind and actively embracing the process of self-love. More guidance on this challenge is in the section "Template and Guide to Write Your Own," on page 40.

EXAMPLES:

Dear Me,

Although this feels kind of weird, it also feels kind of good. I never thought I would write to myself, but the idea is exciting because I know I can be completely honest. Sometimes it's easier to write positive things about other people but not so much myself. But I know I'm a good person. I know I have value, and I know there are a lot of positive things about being me.

For starters, I am an awesome cook. Seriously, I should have been a chef! Maybe it's because I like to follow everything by the letter, including recipes, and so it's really just a matter of following instructions correctly and getting the details right.

But this letter should be about more than cooking. What underlies my love for cooking is that I love to see people enjoying my food. It makes me happy. So I guess that means I'm caring, nurturing, and generous. Yeah, I totally am. I'm also great at giving hugs. If I weren't me, I would want to be hugged by me!

I also love that I've learned to listen more attentively. I used to talk a lot, but ever since I made an effort to listen more actively, I find people want to listen more to what I have to say too. I'm proud of myself for learning that skill.

I have a lot of good qualities, and I know there are more, but I'll write again tomorrow.

Until then, I will sleep well knowing that I am an important and loved person.

Me xo

Dear Me,

Never forget how resilient and resourceful you are in the face of challenges. You can overcome anything and achieve anything you set your mind to with your positive attitude and persistence.

Love,

Me

I am a joyful, positive, inspiring person who brings a smile to peoples' faces.

I love that I have all the skills I need to follow my dreams and live the life I choose. I am committed to myself, my well-being, and to furthering my self-awareness, and I look forward to seeing my goals achieved because I have faith and believe they are possible.

Dear Me,

You are worthy, beloved, valuable beyond measure.

What do you need today? What do you desire today?

As you place your feet upon the ground—the stage for your life—what will you create here today? You are the director of this play and the main character. What is it that you want to have happen today, soon, in the future? What do you look like? How are you dressed? Who are you with? What makes you smile? What soothes you? Paint the canvas of your life with all of these things.

Be still, breathe, and look to the sky. Do you feel your connection to where you came from? Can you carry that with you today and every day? Can you ask for the support you need today?

Where is the care and love for your divine self? Profound self-nurturing is at the very center of all that is to come for you. Eat delicious food, jump in the ocean, say your truth, laugh, rest, find the sunshine.

The divine expresses itself as you on this earth. You are worthy of all the blessings, love, joy, and sunshine every day.

Create it! Today!

Love,
Me

BEFORE YOU WRITE YOUR LETTER...

Complete the following sentences:

1. I would like to write a letter to myself because...

    ....
    ....
    ....

2. After writing this letter, I would like to feel...

    ....
    ....
    ....

3. I will write this letter... (in a journal, on nice paper, etc.)

    ....
    ....
    ....

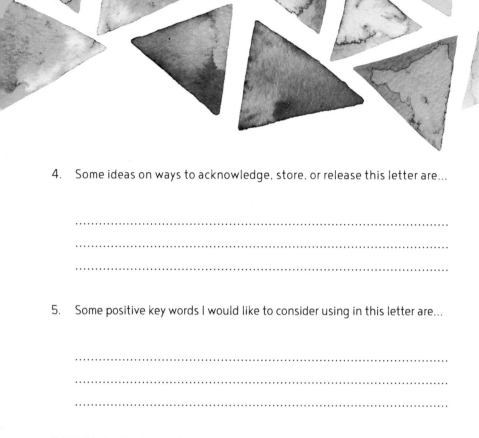

4. Some ideas on ways to acknowledge, store, or release this letter are...

....

....

....

5. Some positive key words I would like to consider using in this letter are...

....

....

....

TEMPLATE AND GUIDE TO WRITE YOUR OWN:

General letter:

1. Dear Me/Name/Nickname...

2. Write how it feels to be writing to yourself. Be honest!

3. Write about your positive qualities and how they add to your life and the lives of others.

4. Write about challenges you have overcome and what you've learned.

5. Write about what you are looking forward to doing, learning, or embracing more fully in your life.

Thirty-day self-love challenge:

1. Create a positive quality word bank—a list of as many positive attributes you can think of that you possess (e.g., generous, kind, positive, inspiring, resourceful, helpful, understanding, determined, resilient, smart, courageous).

2. Every day for thirty days, take a few of these words and create a sentence or two about yourself, like an affirmation of your value and worth (e.g., *I am a kind and generous person who loves to help others. I am smart and courageous in my career and I am rewarded for this*).

3. Whenever you feel down, refer to your word bank, remind yourself of your positive qualities, and write an affirmation you can repeat to yourself regularly or write a longer letter of self-love and acceptance.

....
....
....
....
....
....
....
....
....
....
....
....
....
....
....
....
....
....
....
....
....
....
....
....
....
....
....
....

....
....
....
....
....
....
....
....
....
....
....
....
....
....
....
....
....
....
....
....
....
....
....
....
....
....
....
....
....

DEAR YOUNGER ME

Write a letter of support and guidance to yourself at a younger age, explaining what you know now and giving reassurance.

WHY WRITE TO YOUR YOUNGER SELF?

As opposed to writing to your current self, writing to your younger self allows you to reflect on how far you have come and what you have learned—and pass on any advice you wished you had when you were a certain age in the past. This is a way of acknowledging your growth and being kind and loving to that younger part of you that still exists inside and needs support and nurturing. A letter like this, if chosen to be shared, may also be of help to another person of the same age, allowing them to receive the advice you wish your younger self had had. Although everyone has different life journeys, there are always similarities between us that we can relate to. And if the letter is for your eyes only, then you will find that no matter where you are in life now, you have amassed wisdom and experiences that have allowed you to grow in awareness and that have helped you develop valuable insights you can share with yourself and others. A letter to your younger self can be a great healing tool for self-confidence and to help you move forward.

WHAT TO DO WITH THE LETTER:

As with the letter to your current self, you may wish to keep a special journal or memento box for letters to your younger self, so you can reread them. Writing to yourself regularly is a bit like journaling or keeping a diary, except you are writing directly to yourself as opposed to some other unseen entity.

As this letter is to your past self, you may wish to release it in a more definitive way, such as burning, tearing up and disposing of, or creating a ritual to release the past by also gathering up items you no longer need or want and donating or releasing them in some way too. Or if you like to keep mementos from the past, you could place the letter in a box along with them, as a keepsake.

HOW TO WRITE IT:

Choose an age in the past and write a letter to yourself at that age, as though you are visiting yourself from the future and able to pass on wisdom and advice that will be of help. What would your younger self liked to have known? What would have been of great value to know at that age? Also, acknowledge the positive qualities you possessed at that age and praise your accomplishments. Then, write down what would have helped your younger self move forward with more confidence.

EXAMPLES:

Dear twenty-year-old me (from forty-year-old me).

Happy birthday! Enjoy your celebrations, because pretty soon your life will change forever. Don't worry. It will all work out, and you will enter into a new phase of life that will lead you to follow your heart, and you will discover strength that you never knew you had.

You are about to discover that you are going to be a mother. See this as another journey and adventure for you. Your child will be an amazing gift in your life, and you will have a great relationship as the years go by.

You will have to make a decision next year that will be incredibly difficult, but in your heart, you will know you are making the right one. Don't worry about what other people will think. Just do what you know is right.

As the years pass, look after yourself, not just your child. Your own self-care is just as important. Listen to your own intuition about your health; it is accurate. And get as much sleep as you can. You will need it!

I want you to know that you are intelligent and capable, though you may not have realized this before. You will achieve great things and surprise yourself.

I know you want to work hard to provide for your child, but try to balance your life with relaxation, social opportunities, and doing things you enjoy. Don't let the fun things go.

Don't let fear hold you back. You like to feel safe, but sometimes the greatest experiences come after taking a leap of faith. And enjoy each and every moment. Don't keep rushing ahead to the next one and the next one.

And most of all, be your authentic self.

You are unique and valuable just as you are, so love and appreciate yourself and embrace your true self.

Keep smiling. You have a lot to be grateful for and a lot to look forward to. Know that you will get through the hard times, and your life will continue to surprise you with magical moments and miracles.

Enjoy the journey.

Love,

Me

PS You might as well start using an eye cream now too. ;)

BEFORE YOU WRITE YOUR LETTER...

Complete the following sentences:

1.   I would like to write a letter to my younger self because...

....

....

....

2. After writing this letter, I would like to feel...

....

....

....

3. I will write this letter... (in a journal, on nice paper, etc.)

....

....

....

4. Some ideas on ways to acknowledge, store, or release this letter are...

....

....

....

5. Positive key words that I would like to consider using in this letter are...

....

....

....

6. My favorite color at that age was... (Use it to write or decorate your
    letter.)

    ....

    ....

    ....

TEMPLATE AND GUIDE TO WRITE YOUR OWN:

1. Dear Me/Name/Nickname,

2. State what age you are now, and why you are writing to your younger
    self at a particular age.

3. Talk about what your younger self is going through right now and
    how it fits into the bigger picture of your life.

4. Mention positive attributes and accomplishments that your younger
    self may have forgotten or not seen as significant at that age.

5. Tell your younger self what you would like them to know, how to
    prepare for what is coming next, and a hint about something to look
    forward to.

LETTER #6

DEAR EX

....

Resolve past hurts and give yourself closure
and peace of mind by releasing all that has been
unsaid in a letter to your ex-partner.

WHY WRITE TO YOUR EX-PARTNER?

Writing a letter to an ex-partner is a way to express things
without judgment that you may not have been able to express
verbally during or after the relationship. The letter may be a
healthy release of built-up negative emotion, or it may be a gratitude letter about what you appreciated about the relationship
and what you learned from it. It is a good way to move on in a

more definite way, so you feel like you have been heard and that there is nothing left unsaid, even if the recipient doesn't read the letter. What's important is the release of the emotions, not the reaction to it. This can then create space in your heart and open you up to new possibilities.

WHAT TO DO WITH THE LETTER:

Unless you feel your ex would benefit from receiving the letter, it is usually best to release it in some way, so it signifies an ending and a new beginning and helps to give you closure. So you could burn it, rip it up, and throw it away or discard it respectfully.

HOW TO WRITE IT:

Take some time to reflect upon the relationship, both the positives and negatives. Think back to when it first started and how you felt when you got together, especially if the relationship ended badly. Try to see how it evolved from the beginning to the end without judgment, and become aware of any feelings that come up so you can express them in your letter. When you feel you have a good sense of what you want to express, use the template to guide you through writing your letter, or simply write down whatever comes to mind naturally.

EXAMPLES:

Dear Joel,

I want to thank you—for the laughter, the fun, for showing me I can feel the way I did about you, and for allowing me to open my heart and be able to express how I feel. I am so grateful for how easy it was and how right it felt. I am grateful because meeting you opened my mind and heart to know more fully and truly what I want in life, and it allowed me to dream even bigger and expect more out of my life, so thank you so much.

I wish you the best life and hope you are happy and positive and receive all of your dreams.

With love, light, and more love,
Nancy xxx

Dear Mark,

As I write this letter, tears fill my eyes. The past thirteen years have had beautiful moments and painful ones. I am hovering at the crossroads, afraid to reroute, lingering at the place I have come to know as limbo.

Thank you, Mark, for trying so hard to provide and create what we dreamed of when we first said "I do." Thank you for providing for us, for a beautiful first home, and for the homes and adventures that followed. For taking me places I never would have seen alone. For supporting my ideas to the best of your abilities. For cutting the lawn and working on the house even when it caused you pain. For helping with chores even though you were exhausted from days at work. For our children...above all, thank you for our children.

I wish that I could have healed your pain. It has been at the heart of our falling away. I wish I could help you be happy and whole. I wish we could be joyful together. Letting go of the dreams and promises made so many years ago feels like too much to bear. But staying when things seem to be stagnating is too. Our children deserve happiness. You deserve peace and happiness. I deserve a life filled with love and joy and laughter and undying support. I forgive you. I thank you for what you have given me and what you have tried to give me. As you go forward into life, I hold on to the hope that we can stay friends who continue to support each other through life, especially as parents to our babies. I will always love you and want only the best for you.

With all my love,
Mandy

BEFORE YOU WRITE YOUR LETTER...

Complete the following sentences:

1. I would like to write a letter to my ex because...

   ....

   ....

   ....

2. After writing this letter, I would like to feel...

   ....

   ....

   ....

3. Things I am grateful for from this past relationship are...

    ....
    ....
    ....

4. Things I wish had been expressed that could be expressed now are...

    ....
    ....
    ....

5. I will write this letter... (in a journal, on nice paper, etc.)

    ....
    ....
    ....

6. Some ideas on ways to acknowledge, store, or release this letter are...

    ....
    ....
    ....

TEMPLATE AND GUIDE TO WRITE YOUR OWN:

1. Dear ex [name],

2. Thank this person for their part in your journey.

3. Write down anything you wish to express, stating the emotions you felt/feel.

4. Write down what you learned and what you are grateful for.

5. State that you are giving yourself and them closure and you are now ready to move on.

....

....

....

....

....

....

....

....

....

....

....

....

....

....

....

....

....

....

....

....

....

....

....

....

....

DEAR PET

Express your love and appreciation for a deceased pet who was part of your life (beneficial to help children with the grieving process) or even your existing pet to enhance your bond.

WHY WRITE TO YOUR PET?

Writing a letter to a pet is a great way to acknowledge the important impact and benefit that animals have on our lives. The loss of a pet can be quite upsetting, especially if they were around for a long time, and especially for children, as it can often be their first experience with death. By writing a letter of gratitude, it can help you or your children process what has happened and say good-bye to your pet in a memorable, special way.

WHAT TO DO WITH THE LETTER:

If your pet has recently died, you may like to put the letter with them for their burial or cremation. It could be placed in a special envelope and decorated. Or, if you wish, you could frame the letter alongside a photo of your pet to remember them by, or even place it behind a photo in a frame. If you are keeping any mementos, such as their favorite toy, you could create a memento box with the letter, the toy, and some photos. Or you could simply release it any way you choose.

HOW TO WRITE IT:

If you are sharing this process with children, ask them about their favorite memories of their pet and why they liked having the pet in their life. Talk about the gift that their pet's presence was and how even though the pet is not there anymore, it was a positive experience to have them as part of the family. If you are writing the letter for yourself, take some time to recall the moments you shared and then write all these things down in the letter.

EXAMPLES:

Dear Bella,

Thank you for being our cat. You were cute and fluffy and soft, and I loved stroking your fur and listening to you purr. It made me feel happy and relaxed. I grew up with you, and now that I am getting older, you will no longer be there when I get home from school, but I will always remember walking in the front door and hearing your meow and the way you rubbed up against my leg. We might get a new cat, but you will always be in my memory. You were like a little sister to me.

Thank you for being such a great pet. I will miss you, and I will always love you.

Love,
Kate

Dear Lulu,

I miss sitting with you on the couch after a tiring day, and I miss it even more when I notice stray doggy hairs around the house that have somehow remained, despite my attempts to keep the house clean. You were my friend, my companion, and a trusted confidante, listening to my rambles and worries, and just always being there.

I knew the time would come when I would have to let you go, and though I didn't want to, I knew it was best for you. I didn't want to see you in any pain, and I hope wherever you are now, your spirit is still barking happily and leaping high to catch that tattered, old ball I used to throw for you.

Thanks for being my best friend. I'll never forget you.

Madeleine

BEFORE YOU WRITE YOUR LETTER...

Complete the following sentences:

1.   I would like to write a letter to my pet because...

....

....

....

2. After writing this letter, I would like to feel...

    ....
    ....
    ....

3. If my pet could understand one thing, I would like to tell them...

    ....
    ....
    ....

4. I will write this letter... (in a journal, on nice paper, etc.)

    ....
    ....
    ....

5. Some ideas on ways to acknowledge, store, or release this letter are...

    ....
    ....
    ....

TEMPLATE AND GUIDE TO WRITE YOUR OWN:

1. Dear pet [name],

2. Say why you are writing this letter.

3. Tell them about any memories that make you smile.

4. Tell them how they were an important and valued part of your life.

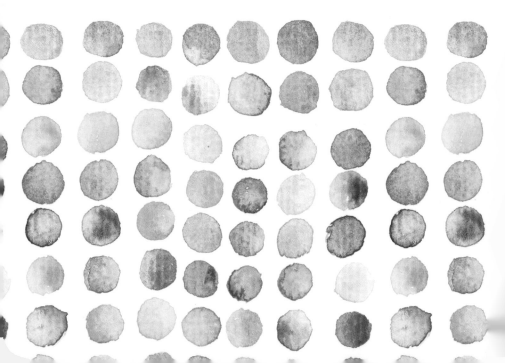

....
....
....
....
....
....
....
....
....
....
....
....
....
....
....
....
....
....
....
....
....
....
....
....
....

DEAR BABY/ FUTURE CHILD

If you are a parent-to-be or wish to be a parent in the future, this letter is to share your hopes, excitement, love, and anticipation for your unborn baby.

WHY WRITE TO YOUR UNBORN BABY OR FUTURE CHILD?

This is a letter to write either when you already know you are expecting or you wish to be now or in the future. Writing to your unborn or future baby is a way to energetically connect with them or with the possibility, and to appreciate their upcoming presence in your life. It is a way for you to connect with the feelings of anticipation and gratitude for the gift of your child's life, and it's a way to express your love and hopes for your child and their future. Writing to a future baby is a great tool for those trying to conceive or going through fertility treatment, or for those not ready or able to have a child yet but who want to do so in the future.

WHAT TO DO WITH THE LETTER:

You can save this letter to give to your child when they are older, or you can put it along with other keepsakes in a baby album or memento box. Or you can simply record it in a journal and write more letters each month or as the urge arises, so you have a series of letters for either your own benefit or to present your child with when they are older. For a child that has not been conceived yet, you may wish to add the letter to a vision board or release it in some way to put your intention out there.

HOW TO WRITE IT:

You may wish to do a brief meditation first, with your hand on yours or your partner's belly, or if you are adopting or using surrogacy, then simply take a few moments to close your eyes, breathe slowly, and feel gratitude for the baby that is on its way. Then put pen to paper and write to your child, telling them how much you are looking forward to meeting them and being their parent. Write about all the things you will teach them and what activities you are looking forward to. Tell them about other family members and pets, or about your home. Acknowledge that they are part of your life already. If you are part of a couple, both of you may wish to write a separate letter and then share it with each other.

EXAMPLES:

Dear Baby,

Most people know me as Rachel, but you will know me as Mommy, or Mom when you're a little older. You are my child and will eventually be a grown adult just like me. But for now, you are my baby. I don't know yet whether you are a boy or a girl. All I know is that you are special, loved, and wanted. I cannot wait to meet you and look after you, to help you grow, learn, and enjoy all the experiences of life.

As I place my hand on my belly, I can feel a little flutter. It's so exciting knowing that a tiny human is growing in my womb, and I wonder things like: Do you have thoughts? Can you hear sounds? Can you feel the vibrations of my voice? I am looking forward to holding your hand for the first time and seeing your face, kissing your forehead, and showering you with care and affection.

One day I might show you this letter, and if you are reading this now with your very own eyes, I want you to know that from the moment I knew you were coming, you were loved. You are loved. You are my child, my blessing, and I will always be here for you.

Love,
Mommy

Dear Future Baby,

Today is February 3, 2017. It's your auntie Lily's birthday today. She is Brandon's mom. You and Brandon will grow up together like Lily and I did, and now we are like sisters. I have been thinking about you a lot lately. I am now ready to be the mother to you that you deserve and give you and your siblings the best, most fun life ever.

We will have so much fun. Our family is a bit crazy, and we have our faults, but I am here to help you learn from us all and become the best you, you can be.

I have also been manifesting the best father for you and husband to me so that our family will grow and learn together.

We are nearly there, my love. I am so excited to meet you.

All my love,
Mommy xxx

Dear Future Surrogate Baby,

I'm writing this letter to connect with you before we start our journey in the coming months. I had the absolute privilege of bringing your little sister into the world a while back, and now, I sit here thinking about the possibility, the dream of you and what you will mean to your fathers, your sister, and to me and my family.

I want you to know that on your journey with me, I promise to protect, nurture, and support you while offering the best possible environment for your thriving.

In that moment when you separate yourself from me, meet the world, and your journey on this beautiful earth begins, when you are scooped up by your fathers after your birth and held by your besotted little sister, I want you to know that I will always hold a place for you in my heart and that I will be filled with the most vibrant gratitude for you choosing me to be your birth mother.

I will watch over you on this journey called life. I will always be waiting in the wings if you ever need me, as my family is your family.

The love I hold inside for you will never wane; there is enough for you, your sister, and my own children. May your journey to your fathers be smooth, easy, and timely, and I look forward to the day I hold you in my arms, see your tiny face, let you grip my finger in your small, warm hand, and let the blessing and gift of you settle inside me.

Love always,
Your birth mother

BEFORE YOU WRITE YOUR LETTER...

Complete the following sentences:

1. I would like to write a letter to my unborn baby or future child because...

    ....
    ....
    ....

2. After writing this letter, I would like to feel...

    ....
    ....
    ....

3. I will write this letter... (in a journal, on nice paper, etc.)

    ....
    ....
    ....

4. Some ideas on ways to acknowledge, store, or release this letter are...

....

....

....

5. Some positive key words I would like to consider using in this letter are...

....

....

....

TEMPLATE AND GUIDE TO WRITE YOUR OWN:

1. Dear Baby [name if you have chosen one]/Future Baby,

2. Introduce yourself as their parent and tell them about yourself.

3. Tell them you are looking forward to meeting them and all the things you are looking forward to.

4. Write about what you wish for their life and future.

5. Tell them you love them and anything else you wish to say.

....

....

....

....

....

....

....

....

....

....

....

....

....

....

....

....

....

....

....

....

....

....

....

....

....

....

LETTER #9

DEAR SON/DAUGHTER

Write a letter to your child or children to give to them on a specific birthday or write one for each year of their childhood.

WHY WRITE TO YOUR SON AND/OR DAUGHTER?

This is one type of letter that may be best to *not* be a secret. It still can be, of course, if there are things you simply want to express to release them from your mind, but if you have positive things to say to one or more of your children, then imagine what a gift it would be for them to receive it. Especially if you have any difficulties in expressing your emotions verbally, a letter can be a good way of showing your children you love them and building up their self-esteem by acknowledging all their positive traits. You could even make it a tradition—a new letter for each birthday.

WHAT TO DO WITH THE LETTER:

You can simply write it on a plain piece of paper and give it to them when you have finished, or you could decorate it and give it to them on a special day to commemorate something in their life. You could even have it framed for display, or depending on the length, you could have it engraved onto a plaque or some other object. You could also consider writing a few at different times and saving them all to give to them on a significant birthday, such as their sixteenth, eighteenth, or twenty-first, or if you have older children, another significant birthday or commemorative date.

HOW TO WRITE IT:

Decide on the reason and purpose of your letter, since this is one you will most likely give to the recipient, and have a clear intention of what you want to say and the benefits for your child. You may wish to look over photos of them to remind you of happy memories, or simply take some quiet time to reflect and write down whatever you wish to express. Depending on the age of your child, what you express and how much will vary, so adjust it according to their level of comprehension and whether it is going to be a one-off letter or one of many.

EXAMPLES:

Dear Son,

I could write a whole book for you, but for now, I'll stick to a short letter.

I am writing to remind you of how important you are in my life and what a special, unique, and talented person you are, and how proud I am of the man you're becoming.

Parents are supposed to teach their children things, but you've taught me things as well. And you've inspired me to dream big and do the best I can in life. You also stimulate my imagination and I love all the fun times we have had reading stories and playing games and running around the yard.

No matter where you go or what you do in life, you can always count on me to be there for you and to support you one hundred percent. I believe in you and your dreams.

Always stay true to yourself, be proud of who you are and what you believe in, and never give up on anything that matters to you.

Live well, look after yourself, make the most of every moment, and do what makes you feel alive and happy.

Love,
Mom

Dear Daughter,

On your thirteenth birthday, I want to say to you how proud I am of you and the young woman you are becoming. As you enter a new phase, I want you to know that I will always be here for you, even if sometimes it feels like I am trying to get in the way. I will only ever want to love and protect and guide you, and I hope we will always be close and be able to talk to each other about anything. You can count on me to be there for you if you need advice without judgment.

Enjoy your day, and be excited about what is to come.

Love always,
Mom

Dear Son,

Today you took your first steps, and I wanted to write a short letter to express how excited I am, both by your progress and by what is to come as you continue to grow and learn. Your favorite food is bananas, you love your red T-shirt, and you love me reading at least three books to you each night.

I look forward to watching more of your steps, as I know each one will be made with enthusiasm and energy, and I hope this continues throughout the rest of your life, because you have a lot to look forward to.

Love,

Dad

BEFORE YOU WRITE YOUR LETTER...

Complete the following sentences:

1. I would like to write a letter to my son and/or daughter because...

    ....
    ....
    ....

2. After writing this letter, I would like to feel...

    ....
    ....
    ....

3. I will write this letter... (in a journal, on nice paper, etc.)

    ....
    ....
    ....

4. Some ideas on ways to acknowledge, store, give, or release this letter are...

....

....

....

5. Some positive key words I would like to consider using in this letter are...

....

....

....

6. My child's favorite color is... (Use it to write or decorate your letter.)

....

....

....

TEMPLATE AND GUIDE TO WRITE YOUR OWN:

1. Dear [child's name],

2. Tell them the reason you are writing to them as opposed to talking to them.

3. Tell them about their positive traits, gifts, and talents.

4. Write about memories and experiences where they have shown these positive traits (e.g., "I remember the time when...").

5. Tell them what having them in your life means to you.

6. Talk about what you wish for them and their future, and how you want them to be happy and follow their dreams.

7. In your own words, tell them you will always be there for them in support and love.

DEAR ILLNESS

Write to a past or present health condition, acknowledging what it has taught you and the positive aspects you choose to make from it to embrace better health and peace of mind.

WHY WRITE TO YOUR PAST OR PRESENT ILLNESS?

When most people think of illness, they think of suffering, and that is understandable, but many who have experienced significant illness can attest to the power of also looking at it in a positive light and seeing what it has taught you or is teaching you. Writing to an illness is a powerful way of acknowledging it as part of your journey but not allowing it to become your identity. This can create wonderful shifts in mind-set that can help you achieve more peace of mind and comfort, and because stress relief is important for health, it may even assist you in improving your health in some ways. You can also write to the illness of someone else who is close to you, in order to deal with feelings of unfairness, worry, and concern, as illness not only affects the sufferer, but those who care about them as well.

WHAT TO DO WITH THE LETTER:

You might like to keep it in your journal as a reminder, so whenever you feel unwell or frustrated, you can read it to remind yourself of your own empowerment. Or you may prefer to discard it via a meaningful release process, such as burning or ripping up, as a way of announcing that you no longer let your illness overwhelm you. What you feel is best will most likely depend on the condition and prognosis you have, but always remember that the mind is a powerful healing tool, and peace of mind can be achieved no matter what you are going through.

HOW TO WRITE IT:

Write or type the letter depending on what is easier for you. If writing or typing is difficult, you may like to have someone you trust assist you by writing it on your behalf as you speak, or you may like to record an audio version of the letter and then have it transcribed.

Acknowledge the condition and how it has impacted your life, but don't dwell on how difficult it is or has been. Think about something you have learned from having the illness, no matter how small. Try to identify something positive that has occurred as a result, even if it is simply meeting friendly, caring health professionals. Take hold of whatever positivity and gratitude you can. You may have or have had a condition that taught you to put yourself first or make more time for self-care and relaxation, or maybe you learned to eat and cook more nutritiously, or learned meditation, or developed a greater understanding of the human body that made you realize how amazing it is. Write it all down, taking the negative aspects of the illness and turning them into positives so you can find the ability to be grateful for the lessons and the unexpected gifts you have received. If you are intent on recovering and regaining your health, you may also like to tell the illness that you have learned the lessons and are grateful for the gifts and no longer require the illness to be present in your life.

EXAMPLES:

Dear Breast Cancer,

I just want to say wow and thank you for the wake-up call you gave me! Although I am still going through my cancer journey, as I am having reconstructive surgery, you helped me realize that I needed to change. I think I was on a self-destruct journey before you arrived to show me I needed to make some adjustments. I was always feeling low, unloved, and unlovable, and I didn't like myself at all. Then you came with a vengeance, shortly after losing my dad to cancer, so I didn't even have time to grieve. It seemed so cruel and I kept asking constantly, "Why me? What have I done wrong to have such a horrible life? Am I really such a bad person?" These were all things that were sent to make me look at why you manifested in my body. After getting over the initial shock and starting treatment, I kept getting feelings to heal myself, and every time I thought about this, I felt calm and peaceful. I was being guided by my body to heal myself from you, Illness, and rediscover who I truly was. This sent me on a path of self-discovery, with lots of crying and forgiving, and for at least six months, you were no longer there and had healed. Then you came back with a vengeance because, although I had done a lot of work forgiving myself and others, I had forgotten the most important lesson that you were trying to teach me: to love myself!!! So after surgery and months of feeling really low, I picked myself up and started to learn how to love myself. I am taking this one day at a time, but I can honestly say, to myself and others, that I do love myself and always will. This hasn't been an easy journey for me, and I still have some way to go, but I would like to thank you from the bottom of my heart for making me realize that I am loved, lovable, and loving. I am good enough.

~ Karen

BEFORE YOU WRITE YOUR LETTER...

Complete the following sentences:

1. I would like to write a letter to my illness because...

    ....
    ....
    ....

2. After writing this letter, I would like to feel...

    ....
    ....
    ....

3. I will write this letter... (in a journal, on nice paper, etc.)

....

....

....

4. Some ideas on ways to acknowledge, store, or release this letter are...

....

....

....

5. Some positive key words I would like to consider using in this letter are...

....

....

....

6. The color I associate with healing is... (Use it to write or decorate your letter.)

....

....

....

TEMPLATE AND GUIDE TO WRITE YOUR OWN:

1. Dear [name of illness],

2. If you are feeling fed up or frustrated, take this opportunity to get it out. Express how you feel to release your emotions, but then be sure to turn it around and look at it in a positive light.

3. If you can see a reason why you believe you got this illness, write it down. If you know a cause or contributing factor, this can help you feel more in control.

4. Tell the illness what it has taught you and how you are stronger for it.

5. Talk about any positives that occurred because of experiencing the illness. It doesn't matter how small.

6. Tell the illness where you wish to go from here. Do you accept it and plan to live each day with as much joy as possible, or are you making changes to help improve your health and recovery? Are you getting better or wanting to, and have decided to no longer let your identity be taken over by the illness? Whatever you feel you want to do and are able to, write it here.

LETTER #11

DEAR MEDICATION/DRUG/ HABIT/ADDICTION

Write to a medication you are weaning off, thanking it for its help while you needed it, or a drug, habit, or addiction, to acknowledge what it taught you and how you are now empowering yourself to live without it.

WHY WRITE TO A MEDICATION, DRUG, OR HABIT?

Similar to writing to an illness, this is a way to acknowledge something that has been part of your journey but that doesn't define who you are. It may be a medication that you no longer require or are weaning off with the guidance of your medical professional, or it may be a substance—such as prescription medication, cigarettes, or a drug that you have been using in an unhealthy way—or a habit or addiction you want to break. By becoming aware of what you have learned, being grateful for any positives that have resulted, and directly stating that you are ready to live a life without it, you can start to prepare or assist your mind to release it from your life. A letter is a valuable tool alongside any other therapies that you may be using.

WHAT TO DO WITH THE LETTER:

You could store it with your medication bottle until you discontinue it, sleep with it under your pillow for a while, or simply discard it in a ritualistic way, to demonstrate your readiness to release the substance or habit from your life.

HOW TO WRITE IT:

If you're coming off a medication, write about how it has helped you get to where you are now and how you are ready for your body to take over and support your health on its own. Think about what the medication did for you and how your body could be able to provide those functions, and believe that it can. If you're addressing a drug or other harmful substance, write about why you started taking it and how it became part of your life. Even though it may be a harmful substance, mention any positives that came from this experience (such as learning to respect your body by giving up this drug, discovering you have people around you who support you, becoming more determined to live a healthier life). The same can be done for a habit or other addiction. Write about how you will support yourself and take care of your mind and body, and how you have everything you need to nourish yourself with healthier options.

EXAMPLES:

Dear Medication,

Thank you for your support over the last five years. Thank you for allowing me to get through each day and live my life. I appreciate how you brought my blood tests back into normal range, so my body could return to a state of balance. I love that you did this for me without any side effects. I am very lucky.

There is a twenty percent chance I can get by without you now, and I would like to be in that twenty percent. So this letter is to let you know that it is time for me to take over your role. I am ready to be my own medication. I now know how to keep my body in balance and will do my best to honor the contribution you have made by maintaining my state of health and balance. I will do this by loving my body and taking care of my physical, emotional, mental, and spiritual needs. I will establish a healthier sleep routine, and I will meditate regularly, knowing that each time I do, it is like a dose of well-being flooding my body. I need only relax, breathe, and enjoy this experience to access my own healing power.

I will enjoy regular exercise and movement, helping me to become stronger. I will nourish my body with healthy natural foods, and I will make time for things I enjoy in life as an expression of self-care.

I will remember the unlimited healing power of my body and know that I have all I require right now for my ideal state of health. So thank you, Medication. I'll take it from here.

Jane

Dear Alcohol,

Letting go of you is like letting go of a friend. But it is one friendship I must leave behind, because although you have been there for me, you have also played a part in my downfall. I was grateful you were there when I needed you, but now that I'm stronger, I no longer need you, and this letter is a way for me to terminate this unhealthy friendship.

Starting today, and when I sign my name at the end of this letter, there is no going back. This is my last communication with you, my final word, our final drink. It is like a resignation letter. I am now moving on to better things and preparing to make the most of my life and honor this body I've been given to carry me through life. I don't intend to waste it anymore.

I have support by my side, and I am no longer too proud to accept any help I can get. I'll take it all. I am ready to move on and start fresh. I no longer require your services. I have all that I need now.

Good-bye to you and my past, and hello to my future.

Jack

BEFORE YOU WRITE YOUR LETTER...

Complete the following sentences:

1. I would like to write a letter to my medication, drug, or habit because...

   ....
   ....
   ....

2. After writing this letter, I would like to feel...

   ....
   ....
   ....

3. I will write this letter... (in a journal, on nice paper, etc.)

   ....
   ....
   ....

4. Some ideas on ways to acknowledge, store, or release this letter are...

....
....
....

5. Some positive key words I would like to consider using in this letter are...

....
....
....

6. When I am free of this substance or addiction, I will celebrate my success by...

....
....
....

TEMPLATE AND GUIDE TO WRITE YOUR OWN:

1. Dear [medication/drug/habit name or name of addiction],

2. Acknowledge why you started this substance or habit.

3. Write how it helped you or what you learned from it and any other positives.

4. Say that you can now take over those needs and help yourself.

5. Mention the ways in which you will look after yourself and nourish your mind and body.

6. Confirm that you will take it from here and are looking forward to being free and healthy.

....
....
....
....
....
....
....
....
....
....
....
....
....
....
....
....
....
....
....
                    ....
                    ....
                    ....
                    ....
                    ....

DEAR AUTHOR / BOOK

Write to a favorite book or author describing how
they've had an impact on you and how the work
brought something positive to your life.

WHY WRITE TO AN AUTHOR OR BOOK?

You can write a letter to an author or book to either send to
the author or to simply acknowledge the impact of the book or
author privately for yourself. Authors do love receiving positive
feedback, so you may wish to share it with them if they are
still living. If a particular book spoke to you or affected you
or your life in some way, this type of letter is a great way to

show gratitude for that. A lot of time is invested into creating a book, and acknowledging the impact is a great reward for both yourself and the author. Whether fiction or nonfiction, books have the power to entertain, enlighten, and inspire, and they can sometimes be symbolic of turning points in our lives.

WHAT TO DO WITH THE LETTER:

Consider sending the letter via email, posting it on social media and tagging the author, posting it on a blog, or even sending it via old-fashioned mail if the author has a mailing address on his or her website. You can also make the letter your own version of a book review and post it on a book retailer website. Reviews are a great way to give back to an author, as they help a book get more exposure. If contacting a particular author seems challenging due to their privacy or security restrictions, you can always send a letter to their agent or publisher to pass on to them.

If you'd rather keep the letter to yourself or if the author is deceased, you could keep a journal especially for letters to the books you read, so you can keep track of books as you read them and what you've learned or why you appreciated them.

If you're in a book club, you could also start a regular letter-writing activity where, at each meeting, you read a letter you've written about the book you're discussing, or you could even start a new book club especially for this purpose.

HOW TO WRITE IT:

Think about books and authors that have had an impact on you, however small or significant, or look through your bookshelves. Perhaps consider one you read when you were recovering from the flu that helped you forget about your symptoms for a few hours, or one that made you laugh for the first time in ages, or one that made you cry but in a good way, or one that really made you think about your own life or inspired you to make a change in your life. If you'd like, make a list of a few, then choose one to start with.

Revisit the book and what you remember about it. Then start writing about all the things you enjoyed, particular scenes or characters, settings, or the style of writing. Mention what you learned and which parts stayed with you or affected you most.

EXAMPLES:

Book:

Dear 1984 by George Orwell,

I am writing to you to say thank you for coming into my life during my teen years. I'm so grateful that the story you told influenced me and had a huge impact on the person I have turned out to be.

From your first line—"It was a bright, cold day in April, and the clocks were striking thirteen."—you had my attention. Here is a quiet, ordinary man, Winston Smith, who doesn't want to conform. Relishing his dreams and memories, he finds the courage, strength, and determination to rebel against the grim authoritarian regime and get what he wants— even at the risk of punishment.

Winston's story grabbed at my emotions and never let go. You see, though I was young, I related to everything Winston was going through in his mind. I'd been a happy, carefree child when my parents migrated to Australia from Europe, but that young-child joy disappeared when I started school and learned very quickly how I didn't fit into the "norm." I spoke a foreign language at home. The food in my lunchbox looked nothing like what the Australian kids ate. My shoes looked cheap.

I turned quiet and kept mostly to myself, though I yearned to be included with all the other girls, to conform and be like them. Your tale about Winston showed me that conforming, doing what others do and thinking as they think, is not always right and, in fact, can be detrimental. *You gave me the courage to bring out of hiding the carefree, happy side of me that looks at life with optimism. You gave me the strength and determination to stand up for what I believe is right, even if it means standing alone.*

I thank you for showing me I can be me.

Regards,
Enisa

Author:

Dear Mr. Roald Dahl,

Ever since I started reading your books to my children, you've been a part of my life.

My children adored your books. I mean, seriously, who wouldn't like to meet talking crickets and a ladybug that inhabit a giant peach or get lifted away in the night to the land of giants with the chance to change their bad habits?

At the same time, your macabre mind took

me to places I didn't think I wanted to go. In "Skin," you showed us the depths of depravity people will go to take what they want.

But still I couldn't get enough of your stories. When the BFG hit the big screen, I was there. I wish I'd had the chance to chat with you over a drink in a corner pub, to find out where your ideas came from. Since that's not possible, I'll have to console myself by delving back into your imaginary world. But I wonder: Where did it all begin?

Sincerely,
Ann

BEFORE YOU WRITE YOUR LETTER...

Complete the following sentences:

1. I would like to write a letter to an author or book because...

....

....

....

2. After writing this letter, I would like to feel...

....
....
....

3. I will write this letter... (in a journal, on nice paper, etc.)

....
....
....

4. Some ideas on ways to acknowledge, store, or give this letter are...

....
....
....

5. Some positive key words I would like to consider using in this letter are...

....
....
....

6. The significant words, symbols, or imagery I associate with this book are... (Consider using them in creative ways in the letter or to decorate your letter.)

....

....

....

TEMPLATE AND GUIDE TO WRITE YOUR OWN:

1. Dear [author name or book title],

2. Tell them why you are writing this letter.

3. If a book, write about what you liked about it, your favorite scenes and characters, or the information you learned and how it impacted your life.

4. If an author, tell them what you liked about one (or more) of their books and maybe even about the time in your life when you read it, how it had an impact, and that you are grateful for their words.

5. Add any other messages or words you wish to express, then sign it with your name (and if sending the letter, make sure you have a way for them to reply via email, mail, or social media should they wish to do so).

....
....
....
....
....
....
....
....
....
....
....
....
....
....
....
....
....
....
....
....
....
....
....
....
....
....
....

LETTER #13

DEAR UNIVERSE/GOD

Write to your preferred higher power or entity, either a letter of gratitude for what you have in your life, your hopes and wishes, or a letter containing questions you have.

WHY WRITE TO THE UNIVERSE OR A HIGHER POWER?

This is a great letter for many different purposes: for when you want to release, express, or ask things in a more general way. You can adjust the letter and the name you address it to according to your beliefs (e.g., Dear God, Dear Source, or any other specific name you associate with prayer, religion, or spirituality). A universe letter can be quite powerful because it is a way to directly state any desires or dreams and put them out there, which, when accompanied by trust and belief, creates a more positive mind-set to help you receive more of what you want in your life. It can also be beneficial and empowering to simply give gratitude for your many blessings in life, which puts you in a happier state of mind.

Writing questions to the universe can also be a powerful exercise. It can enhance your intuition, and you may find that the answers come to you as you write or appear a day or so later. There is infinite wisdom available to us, and you may just discover some interesting answers and concepts you had not yet been aware of.

WHAT TO DO WITH THE LETTER:

You can symbolically give the letter to the universe by burning it and watching the smoke drift up to the sky, or letting pieces of it float in a body of water (use recycled paper made of natural materials if you want to do this), or burying it, keeping it in a special *Letters to the Universe* journal, file, or mailbox, or sleep with it under your pillow for a few nights. You can even make a digital copy and email it to a special Universe email address that you set up especially for yourself for any letters or requests to the universe, and you can also create an autoreply to acknowledge that your letter or request has been received and granted.

If you write a letter with questions, you may wish to keep the letter awhile instead of discarding, so you can revisit the questions to see if any answers have appeared in your mind. Or write a separate letter just for your questions.

A fun idea is to hold a Letters to the Universe Party with some friends, whereby each person brings their letter to the universe (or writes them at the party), and you all release the letters together in a special ritual to add more energy and power to the process, enhancing your relationships with your friends at the same time. Depending on the contents of the letter, you may even wish to read your letter to the group first.

HOW TO WRITE IT:

Decide what the purpose of your letter is. You may like to write a few different letters for different purposes or one letter containing everything you wish to express. Get relaxed and make sure you have some peace and quiet, so you can really think and feel what it is you wish to say. Regardless of what the purpose is, it is always a good idea to start with writing about what you are grateful for or what you appreciate in your life. Write to the universe as though it is a trusted friend and guide there to assist you in any way you like. If you are writing to declare your desire to manifest certain things in your life, do it from a place of gratitude, not need, as this puts you in a more positive and receptive frame of mind. Use the examples to inspire you, and write what you love about your life, what you are looking forward to, and any questions you have.

If you want to write a letter with questions, think about any questions that have been weighing on your mind or anything you would like to know the answers to, whether about yourself and your situation or broader questions about the world. After you've written your questions, you can go back to the first one and see if any answers come to you, and if so, don't censor or judge them—just let the words flow. If not, leave the questions under your pillow or in a journal, and go back to them the next day or so and see if the answers are any clearer.

EXAMPLES:

General letter:

Dear Universe,

I would just like to say how grateful I am for all that I have in my life—my family, friends, career, and health. I am truly blessed, and I thank you.

I would also like to say thanks for the wonderful surprises and blessings coming my way. I trust that you know when the time is right for everything, and I look forward to seeing how my life unfolds. I am especially looking forward to becoming more financially stable and being able to travel and have new experiences. I'm also looking forward to being in a committed relationship that enriches my life and to being able to be a supportive partner to someone special. This year is turning out very interesting, and although there are ups and downs, I always know that the ups outweigh the downs and that I always have the strength and resilience to keep going and moving forward. Thank you for all that you provide. I am excited to see what great things are around the corner for me.

Love,
Lea

Q&A letter:

Dear Universe,

Question: *Who are we?*

Answer: *We are the perception of who we are. We are perception itself. And the perception of who we are is forever changing because the perception of who we are now is very different* *from the perception of who we were before and who we are later.*

Question: *Why are we?*

Answer: *Purpose is why we are. Purpose can and will change depending on the situation. Our purpose in life is totally up to us to decide. We are entitled to seek our own destinies.*

~From Tristan

Dear Universe,

Question: *Is our destiny preplanned or do we have control to choose our future?*

Answer: *Destiny is always changing depending on your thoughts, attitudes, emotions, and perceptions. There is a big picture for your life, but there is also freewill. You can affect outcomes by changing your thoughts to align with what you desire. Trust in how your life is unfolding, but also follow your intuition and do what feels right for you.*

~From Julia

BEFORE YOU WRITE YOUR LETTER...

Complete the following sentences:

1. I would like to write a letter to the universe or a higher power because...

    ....
    ....
    ....

2. After writing this letter, I would like to feel...

    ....
    ....
    ....

3. I will write this letter... (in a journal, on nice paper, etc.)

    ....
    ....
    ....

4. Some ideas on ways to acknowledge, store, or release this letter are...

....

....

....

5. Some positive key words I would like to consider using in this letter are...

....

....

....

6. The colors that might represent my dreams, what I am grateful for, or my questions are... (Use these to write or decorate your letter.)

....

....

....

TEMPLATE AND GUIDE TO WRITE YOUR OWN:

Template 1

A general letter of gratitude and/or desires you wish to manifest

1. Dear [Universe or other preferred name],

2. Thank the universe for all your blessings, either in general, or in specific detail.

3. Tell the universe the reason for writing this letter, state any desires you would like to manifest in your life, and write about how you will feel when these are in your life.

4. Thank the universe for listening and for looking out for you and helping you along your life journey.

Template 2

A letter of questions or situations you wish to find answers to or resolve

1. Dear [Universe or other preferred name],

2. Thank the universe for all your blessings, either in general, or in specific detail.

3. Tell the universe the reason for writing this letter, and state any questions or concerns that are on your mind and that you are open to receiving any insight or answers. If answers start to come as soon as you write the questions, let them flow and trust what comes from your pen. If they don't, don't force anything, just move on to the next question or conclude your letter and revisit the questions later. You may like to keep the letter under your pillow or next to your bed and review the questions the next day.

4. Thank the universe for listening and for looking out for you and helping you along your life journey.

....
....
....
....
....
....
....
....
....
....
....
....
....
....
....
....
....
....
....
....
....
....
....
....
....
....

....
....
....
....
....
....
....
....
....
....
....
....
....
....
....
....
....
....
....
....
....
....
....
....
....
....
....
....
....

LETTER #14

DEAR EVERYONE

Write a letter to the masses, people who have something in common with you, in order to help and inspire (e.g., those with the same health condition, recovering from the same addiction, or those going through grief).

WHY WRITE TO EVERYONE?

You may have seen "open letters" posted online, letters that are shared with a large number of people in the hope of educating and enlightening or offering advice or an opinion on a certain topic. This technique can also be a way to thank a certain group of people and express deep gratitude, for example by writing to medical personnel, teachers, or anyone else who offers a valuable service to society. Writing a Dear Everyone letter can be a way to have a positive impact on certain people, offer inspiration and hope, guidance, or insight into a personal experience, so this letter is usually not a secret letter. However, you can do a version of this letter that is secret if the purpose is for you to express pent-up emotions or frustrations about something in order to release them and make way for a fresh, positive perspective.

WHAT TO DO WITH THE LETTER:

If you want to write a secret version of this letter as a form of emotional release, after you have finished, it would be best to symbolically dispose of it in some way.

For a public letter, the best option is to post it online on a blog and/or social media. If you do so, add the hashtag #secret-lettersproject if you would like the possibility of your letter being shared through our community.

For businesses or anyone with an online presence or database, if your letter relates to your clients or their needs, you could send the letter via your email newsletter to subscribers.

Depending on your letter's topic, you could even print out copies and distribute it to relevant organizations, charities, or businesses to increase exposure.

HOW TO WRITE IT:

Have a clear intention for the purpose of your letter. If you feel it is more to express your own emotions or opinions, think carefully about whether sharing it publicly would be beneficial for you and/or others. If you can see that it could have a positive impact on certain people, then that is the main aim of this type of letter.

Make sure you know how you want the target audience to feel after reading your letter or what you want them to get out of it, and then base your words on achieving that aim. For example, you might want them to feel inspired, hopeful, and enthusiastic about something, or you might want them to become more informed or aware about a certain topic, especially if written from a lesser-known viewpoint.

Write down what you wish to express and why you are expressing it, and finish it off with a positive statement that will leave an impact on the reader.

EXAMPLES:

Letter ideas:

Dear Grieving One
Dear Lonely
Dear Country

Dear World
Dear Alcoholics
Dear New Mothers
Dear New Fathers
Dear Cancer Warriors
Dear Fellow Entrepreneur
Dear Aspiring Author
Dear Survivors

Letter examples:

Dear Heartbroken,

I know you are hurting and it feels unbearable, like something has just been ripped out of the book of your life or the ground has been taken out from under your feet. I've been there too. I also felt like it wouldn't get any better or that getting another chance to experience something great would not be possible. But I promise you it is. It is always possible. You might not be able to see that now, and I understand that too, so it's okay. Take your time and allow yourself to feel all the emotions that come through you. They are like water, flowing and fluid, and will keep moving. They are not set in stone. They will pass through, strengthen you, and eventually give you perspective and understanding. The best way through is to just experience it, take it one hour, or even one moment, at a time. Moments pass—time passes, and things do get easier. Better even. So stay tuned for that and for the possibilities that can arise from this difficult time, even though you want it all to be over right now and for things to go back to the way they were. Take notice of what was good about your experience. If you loved and lost, remember that you got to love in the first place. Not everyone gets that. Yes, it makes the loss more painful, but it also makes the memories sweeter. And memories are what life is all about, so keep going, be kind to yourself, give yourself time, and know that you will go on to make more amazing memories than you ever even imagined.

xo,

from someone who has loved and lost too

A personal letter from the author:

Dear Aspiring Author,

If you're just starting out writing your first book or maybe your second, remember one thing: every successful writer has been exactly where you are.

Everyone starts somehow, but what makes a successful writer different is that they finished the book; they saw it through till "The End" and felt that satisfaction of completion. If you've written and you write, that makes you a writer.

So always see yourself as a writer and as successful, because as you go through your writing and publishing journey, you will find that a lot of it is as much about your attitude as it is about your ability. Proudly tell people what you do and give yourself a pat on the back for doing something that many dream of but never actually do.

Get connected with other writers and writing organizations; become part of the industry. You will find help and support, knowledge and opportunities, and even great friends. Learn your craft and practice. Every word you write, every sentence, every page, every chapter, every book is teaching you something. You get better as you go along, and you learn more about yourself and your ideas, your style and your voice the more you write. If you love writing, make it a priority and put regular writing time into your schedule. Most writers started when they had other responsibilities and commitments, but they made time to write because they had the passion for it.

Make your book the best it can be, but let go of perfectionism. Focus on getting the words out and doing the best you can. Write it, edit it, get some outside feedback and/or professional editing help, revise and edit again, and know that, at some point, you have done all you can do for now and it is time to take it to that next step of either looking for publication, self-publishing, or moving on to a new book.

Remember all five senses when writing a scene. This doesn't mean that every description must use all five senses; it just means that you take the time to be creative in how you describe what is happening. And keep practicing the "show, don't tell" concept. Don't always tell the reader what is happening; show them what it looks or feels like as if they were right there, experiencing it themselves.

Come up with interesting and unique characters, and be careful not to overuse stereotypes. Make an effort to show the diversity of life in both people and experiences.

Research your market, the readers of your type of book, and figure out what makes yours both suitable for that readership and unique in the marketplace. Come up with a one- or two-sentence hook (a tagline) so you can sum up your book concisely. This will help with both pitching your book to publishers or agents and also when people ask, "What is your book about?"

If you want to get published, and published again, don't give up. Readers will always want stories, and if you believe in yours, then keep going. But don't get too focused on one book. Keep writing more.

And stay true to your own voice and style. Don't let your distinctive voice be dulled down by overediting or trying to sound like someone else.

Most of all, enjoy what you write. If you're not enjoying it, try something new, and don't be afraid to start over. And never forget the reason you write, because when challenges come up in your writing journey, it helps to remember the big picture and stay focused on your passion. Know that whatever happens, you are following your dream and doing what you love, and that is what life is about.

Keep writing,
Juliet

BEFORE YOU WRITE YOUR LETTER...

Complete the following sentences:

1. I would like to write a letter to everyone because...

    ....
    ....
    ....

2. After writing this letter, I would like to feel...

    ....
    ....
    ....

3. I will write this letter... (on nice paper, online, as a Word document for printing, etc.)

....
....
....

4. Some ideas on ways to release this letter or to share this letter with as many people as possible are...

....
....
....

5. After reading this letter, I would like other people to feel...

....
....
....

TEMPLATE AND GUIDE TO WRITE YOUR OWN:

1.   Dear [name of group],

2.   State your purpose for this letter.

3.   Talk about your experiences with this particular topic.

4.   Write what you would like readers to know.

5.   Finish with a positive and memorable statement.

....

....

....

....

....

....

....

....

....

....

....

....

....

....

....

....

....

....

....

....

....

....

....

....

....

....

....

....
....
....
....
....
....
....
....
....
....
....
....
....
....
....
....
....
....
....
....
....
....
....
....
....
....
....

LETTER #15

DEAR EVENT

....

If there's a significant event that changed your life,
write to it and explain how it changed your life, both the
positives and negatives, to release emotions and move
forward from the past.

WHY WRITE TO AN EVENT?

Writing to an event is a powerful and cathartic way to express
or process any emotions around an event that changed your life
or had a big impact. It could be a positive event or a traumatic
event, but what matters is your response to it, how you would
like to acknowledge its impact on your life, and how you choose

to move forward with strength and positivity. It can be a great transitional tool to clear away the past and step forward into a new life.

WHAT TO DO WITH THE LETTER:

If the letter could be of help to others who have also experienced the same event, then consider writing it as a version of the Dear Everyone letter and sharing it publicly. If it is more for your own healing or empowerment, then you could include it in your letters journal or release it from your life via a ritual that involves burning the letter or discarding it in some way.

HOW TO WRITE IT:

If you're writing about a positive event, recall the memory and write about why it was significant to you and what sort of an impact it had on your life, as well as the person you have now become because of it.

If you're writing about a difficult time, ask a trusted friend or a professional to help you if you need it, or take some quiet time to reflect and process the experience. Then, write down anything you need to express about your emotions, your reactions to the experience, the impact it had on your life, and even if it was difficult, any positives that came from it, beneficial things you learned as a result, or new and positive experiences it led you toward.

EXAMPLES:

Dear Wedding Day,

I am writing to acknowledge this day in my own way, because although the photos and the memories are always there, sometimes words are best to remind us of things. And as I go through my life, and specifically my marriage, I always want to remember the significance of this day.

A wedding is only one day out of a lifetime, but for me, for us, it signals the start of a new life, a life we have chosen to live together. It's the marriage that is most important, not the fancy dresses and flowers and food, but the memories of my wedding day will serve as a reminder of how lucky I am to have found someone to share my life with.

When things get difficult in life, as they sometimes do, and there are ups and downs, I want to remember the simple fact that love is stronger than anything, and in the grand scheme of things, that is all that matters. With love, understanding, acceptance, and commitment, we can get through anything. So when I look at the photos of the dresses, the flowers, the food, I won't just remember a great day that was had by all, especially us. I will remember this simple fact, and it will help to keep me, and us, going strong and growing strong together.

So thank you, Wedding Day, for this gift, and for what you signify. I am so grateful to love and be loved.

Claire

Dear Accident,

You are not something I wish to remember exactly, but I wish to acknowledge the positive that came from the negative. Because even though you were traumatic, without you, I would not have certain things I now have. I would not have the extra strength of mind and body that I now have, thanks to the determination and persistence that was required to get through my recovery, which led to me becoming even stronger than before. I would not have a great new friend who I met during my recovery, and I would not have the memories of those caring people who helped me along the way. I was able to see and experience how many wonderful people there are in the world and what a difference one or two people can make. So for that, I am grateful, and even though it was a difficult time, my life is better now having been through the experience.

Ben

BEFORE YOU WRITE YOUR LETTER...

Complete the following sentences:

1. I would like to write a letter to an event because...

    ....
    ....
    ....

2. After writing this letter, I would like to feel...

    ....
    ....
    ....

3. I will write this letter... (in a journal, on nice paper, etc.)

....

....

....

4. Some ideas on ways to acknowledge, store, or release this letter are...

....

....

....

5. Some positive key words I would like to consider using in this letter are...

....

....

....

6. Some positive qualities I developed or strengthened by going through this event are...

....

....

....

TEMPLATE AND GUIDE TO WRITE YOUR OWN:

1. Dear [event name],

2. Write about why the event was significant for you and why you are writing this letter.

3. Write about the details of how it had an impact and how you felt during and after the event.

4. Write what you learned and any positives that occurred as a result (e.g., made a new friend, witnessed caring people helping others, developed more resilience, recognized what is really important in life, discovered a new career path or purpose).

5. Write about how you plan to move forward in life now that you've had this experience.

....
....
....
....
....
....
....
....
....
....
....
....
....
....
....
....
....
....
....
....
....
....
....
....
....
....
....
....
....
....

LETTER #16

DEAR HOME / TOWN / CITY

Moving out of your beloved family home or the town or city you've been living in? Write a thank-you letter reminiscing about all the pleasant memories you had there. Or write to your future home or location, anticipating all the new memories you will create, or write to your current home or location as a letter of gratitude for what you have.

WHY WRITE TO YOUR HOME OR LOCATION?

Even though a place is not a person, it forms part of a person's life and experiences and can often be associated with signifi-cant memories that shape their life. Writing to a past, current, or future home or location is a way to acknowledge this important part of our living environment and to document and show gratitude for the experiences we associate with it. It can also simply be a gratitude letter for having a roof over your head. This type of letter can also be used if you are looking for the ideal home or new town but haven't found it yet. Try writing to your ideal future home and write down everything you would like about it as a tool to help you find the right home for you.

WHAT TO DO WITH THE LETTER:

If you're writing to your current home, you could frame the letter and display it somewhere prominent or special. For a past home or one you are moving out of, you could bury it in the yard or even pencil it on a wall before painting over it, or just release it in any way you prefer. For a future home, consider sending it in the mail to yourself at your new address, frame it and display it once you move in, keep it in a memento box, or release it.

HOW TO WRITE IT:

For a current home or if you are preparing to move, walk around your home and jot down memories from the various rooms and also things you like about each room. The same goes for a location you might want to write to—walk or drive around to your favorite spots. Then formulate it into a letter to acknowledge all these aspects and memories and feel appreciation for them.

For a future home, if you can visit or know what it looks like, go through each room (physically or via photos or memory) and imagine how you will arrange your things and decorate it, and what experiences you look forward to in each part of the house. Then write it in your letter of excited anticipation for your new home.

EXAMPLES:

To My Future Home,

As I stand at this crossroad, I'm still not sure where you are. But thank you for leading me to you. I am so grateful for you. From the perfect shades of turquoise and taupe on the walls to the large windows that light streams into and the nearby body of water where the kids and I go to unwind, I adore everything about you. Thank you for the inviting warmth and love that you hold. Thank you for giving my loves a beautiful place to form memories.

I love that you are spaciously laid out but not too large. I love that you were designed to be an efficient space with pullout drawers and nooks for our laptops and books.

Your bathroom is clean and relaxing, and the beautiful silver fixtures are such a nice touch. I especially love the garden tub and the tile on the floor.

The bedrooms are so surprisingly spacious and bright with large windows. The kids love having room for all their toys and books, and are excited by their new home.

The kitchen—thank you, Home, for giving me my dream kitchen with room for all of us to eat and make food together. This kitchen is the heart of our home. I love how it flows into the main living room, so we can all sing and dance or watch TV while making dinner. Your layout is wonderful. We are so easily connected. Thank you for feeling like home.

You even have a sweet, finished basement to snuggle in during storms and a studio for my painting and storage needs! This was such a perfect surprise for no increased cost. And thank you for having an included washer and dryer. My piles of laundry appreciate you!

I love that there is a pool and an area for cooking out, a patio, and a small lawn area for the kids to play with their friends. I'm so grateful that I don't have to maintain the lawn or fix problems on my own! I love that all my problems are resolved quickly and efficiently and by someone else, so I never have to worry.

The gym! You save me so much money and help me maintain my health by offering this perfect gym and classes for free. It's perfect, more than I ever expected.

Also, thank you for the garage, so we are able to stay warm and dry! I was so worried about digging out of the snow, but it is handled.

Thank you for keeping us dry and warm, for the inexpensive cable and Internet, for being so close to my babies' school. Thank you for the bringing my family a safe place to be happy together. You are better than I ever imagined. Thank you, universe, for looking out for me!

~Mandy

BEFORE YOU WRITE YOUR LETTER...

Complete the following sentences:

1. I would like to write a letter to my home because...

    ....
    ....
    ....

2. After writing this letter, I would like to feel...

    ....
    ....
    ....

3. I will write this letter... (in a journal, on nice paper, etc.)

    ....
    ....
    ....

4. Some ideas on ways to acknowledge, store, or release this letter are...

....
....
....

5. Some positive key words I would like to consider using in this letter are...

....
....
....

6. My favorite memory in this home or something significant I look forward to in my new home is...

....
....
....

TEMPLATE AND GUIDE TO WRITE YOUR OWN:

1.   Dear Home,

2.   State your purpose for writing the letter.

3.   Write why you are grateful for the home.

4.   Write what parts you like best about it.

5.   Write about the experiences and memories you had, enjoy having, or are looking forward to.

6.   Finish up with how this house had an impact on you and what is next for your living environment and life.

LETTER #17:

DEAR SONG

....

Write to a song or piece of music that you associate
with strong memories or emotions, to give gratitude
for the music and/or lyrics and its impact on your life
or memories it triggers.

WHY WRITE TO A SONG?

Music is powerful and can elicit strong emotions and memories,
just like a certain scent can. It's amazing how you can hear a
song you haven't heard for a long time and yet still remember the
lyrics or feel like you're back in an earlier time when the song
was playing, bringing back memories. Writing to a song is a good

way of reminiscing about your life and significant moments while also acknowledging the songwriter, singer(s), musicians, and composer.

WHAT TO DO WITH THE LETTER:

You can simply release it in any way you wish, keep it in a "memorable songs" journal, a memento box, a photo album along with pictures from the time in your life you associate it with, or even post it online as a tribute to the particular song.

HOW TO WRITE IT:

Make a list of either your favorite songs and/or significant and memorable moments in your life and the music you associate with them. Listen to the song and jot down emotions and memories that come up; then write your letter.

EXAMPLES:

Dear "Hero" by Mariah Carey,

I enjoyed listening to you when you first came out but didn't know how much impact a song could have until I went through heartbreak. I listened to you over and over until the lyrics sunk in, until I believed that I did have the strength to keep going, that I would be okay on my own, and that I could rely on myself and be my own hero. Years later, whenever I hear this song, I still remember that. Thank you.

Jill

Dear "Kiss From a Rose" by Seal,

Apart from being a great song, you were a sign for me that there was something more to this worldly existence than only what we could see. When you played at the moment I was proposed to by my fiancé, I had no idea that less than two years later, you would come onto the radio at the exact moment I drove into the cemetery to visit his grave. I'll never forget the goose bumps and also how appropriate the song title now seemed to be.

Emily

Dear "Peggy Sue" by Buddy Holly and the Crickets,

There was a day back in the fifties when I heard you, and every time I hear the song now, even with my old, failing ears, I am transported back in time. Because it was on that day I decided I wanted to marry my darling Margaret. Somehow, you gave me the confidence to propose, and she said yes. And now, as we are nearing the end of our lives, I would like to say many thanks for this charming memory that I will always cherish.

Bill

BEFORE YOU WRITE YOUR LETTER...

Complete the following sentences:

1. I would like to write a letter to a song because...

....

....

....

2. After writing this letter, I would like to feel...

....
....
....

3. I will write this letter... (in a journal, on nice paper, etc.)

....
....
....

4. Some ideas on ways to acknowledge, store, or release this letter are...

....
....
....

5. The emotions this song triggers are...

....
....
....

6. Some significant memories I associate with this song are...

    ....
    ....
    ....

TEMPLATE AND GUIDE TO WRITE YOUR OWN:

1. Dear [song name and artist/songwriter/composer],

2. State your purpose for writing the letter.

3. Write why you are grateful for the song.

4. Write what you like best about it.

5. Write about the experiences and memories you associate with this song.

....

....

....

....

....

....

....

....

....

....

....

....

....

....

....

....

....

....

....

....

....

....

....

....

....

....

DEAR SPOUSE/PARTNER

Write to your current partner to express gratitude, acknowledge memories or milestones, or to express difficult emotions that may be challenging to express face-to-face.

WHY WRITE TO YOUR SPOUSE OR PARTNER?

Writing down any thoughts or feelings about your partner and relationship that are weighing on your mind can be helpful to assist in communication and conflict resolution and to avoid resentments building up. It can be a way of making sense of what you are feeling or going through, so you can either share it with your partner or allow yourself to become more aware and prepared for a face-to-face discussion.

Writing a gratitude letter can also be a great bonding activity for couples to do with each other.

WHAT TO DO WITH THE LETTER:

You can simply release it in any way you wish, write it in this journal, keep it in a memento box if it's a gratitude letter, or share it with your partner.

HOW TO WRITE IT:

Decide why you are writing this letter and what you would like the benefit to be. Also decide if it is for your benefit or something that would be helpful to share with your partner.

EXAMPLES:

Dear Max,

I love you no matter what. You are an important part of my life, and I will always be here for you. This letter is simply a way for me to express some things that have been weighing on my mind that I would like to share with you.

Since taking your new job, you have been so busy, and I understand you are trying to do the best you can, and I'm thankful for that. But I sometimes feel like it takes priority over our relationship, and I miss spending the same amount of time with you as we used to.

I would love it if we could perhaps schedule some date days or date nights, instead of trying to squeeze in time together, so we can more easily nourish and maintain the wonderful relationship we have. I would also love if during these times we don't keep checking our phones and we allow ourselves to be attentive and focused on each other,

I feel this would help a lot, and I would really love to spend more time with you and do some of the things we've always wanted to do.

Thanks for being part of my life,
Kate

Dear Belinda,

I just wanted to express how grateful I am to have you as my wife. On this day, our first anniversary, I am reminded of our wedding day and how much fun we had, but mostly, how elated I was to finally hear you say, "I do." I am a lucky man to have such a caring, considerate, loving, and positive wife, who brings joy and laughter to my life each day. I look forward to our next year together and many more after that. We have some amazing times ahead of us.

I love you and always will,
Sean

BEFORE YOU WRITE YOUR LETTER...

Complete the following sentences:

1. I would like to write a letter to my partner because...

    ....

    ....

    ....

2. After writing this letter, I would like to feel...

    ....

    ....

    ....

3. I will write this letter... (in a journal, on nice paper, etc.)

    ....

    ....

    ....

4. Some ideas on ways to acknowledge, store, release, or share this letter are...

....

....

....

5. The emotions I am feeling and wish to express are...

....

....

....

TEMPLATE AND GUIDE TO WRITE YOUR OWN:

1. Dear [partner name],

2. State your purpose for writing the letter.

3. Write why you are grateful for your partner.

4. Write what you are feeling and wish to express.

5. Write what you would like this letter to accomplish.

LETTER #19

DEAR FRIEND/RELATIVE

Is there a person in your life you need to express something to? A friend, a parent, a sibling, a relative, a colleague, or someone you admire? Write to them, either to give them the letter, or to simply release your emotions for yourself.

WHY WRITE TO A FRIEND, RELATIVE, OR OTHER PERSON?

Sometimes the written word is an easier way to express what may be difficult face-to-face or verbally. If there are challenging emotions to express, a letter can be a way of being heard clearly without any interruptions, whether you give the letter to the person or not. It can help to make sense of any conflict and also be a way to offer forgiveness or acceptance. It can also be a letter of admiration or gratitude for a person in your life, whether that person is someone you know well or someone who has simply had some kind of impact, no matter how big or small.

WHAT TO DO WITH THE LETTER:

In some cases, you can give the person the letter if it would be beneficial to do so, or you may store it in a special place, keep it in a journal, or release it in a ceremonial way.

HOW TO WRITE IT:

Think of someone you know or have met who you would like to express something to or something you would like to release any emotions about. You don't have to give anyone this letter. Even if it's positive and complimentary, if you don't feel comfortable sharing it, it can still be a powerful tool for healing, gratitude, and even manifestation of more fulfilling interactions and relationships.

State your reason for writing the letter and then allow yourself to honestly express any emotions or thoughts, and also acknowledge what is great about this person and that you wish them well in life.

EXAMPLES:

Dear Annie,

I know we've had our fair share of difficulties over the years, and we've clashed and disagreed and held resentment and hard feelings, but you're still my sister. I am writing this letter to put an end to those resentments and hard feelings, because I don't wish to feel that anymore, and I want to get on with living and enjoying my life. So even if you don't feel the same, I have decided to let things go, to accept things the way they are, to not judge you or try to be right all the time. I am letting that go. I am moving forward with love and acceptance and the hope that our relationship will improve. If not, then I will at least no longer allow it to have such an impact on my life, as it has over the years. So I forgive you, I forgive myself, and I wish us both well in doing what each we believe is right for ourselves.

Your sister,
Sally

Dear Natalie,

I forgive you for what you did and no longer wish to feel this pain, so I am writing today to let you go. What's done is done, and although things can never go back to the way they were before, I hope we can both move on with peace of mind.

Despite your mistake, you are a great person and I know you didn't mean to hurt me, so I forgive you. I am okay. I am taking steps to create a new life for myself now that we are apart.

And I don't feel angry anymore. I only wish you well and hope you are able to enjoy your life and be the courageous person that you are. Thank you for being part of my life. Even though it was only temporary, I am glad you were a part of it.

All the best,
James

BEFORE YOU WRITE YOUR LETTER...

Complete the following sentences:

1. I would like to write a letter to my friend or relative because...

    ....
    ....
    ....

2. After writing this letter, I would like to feel...

    ....
    ....
    ....

3. I will write this letter... (in a journal, on nice paper, etc.)

    ....
    ....
    ....

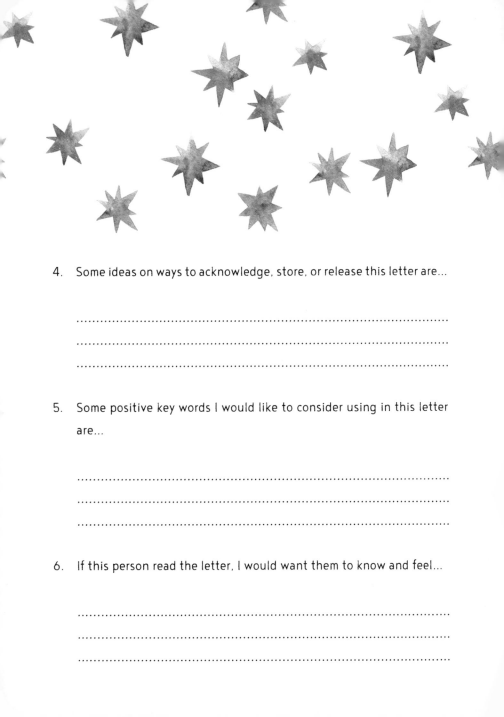

4. Some ideas on ways to acknowledge, store, or release this letter are...

    ....
    ....
    ....

5. Some positive key words I would like to consider using in this letter
    are...

    ....
    ....
    ....

6. If this person read the letter, I would want them to know and feel...

    ....
    ....
    ....

TEMPLATE AND GUIDE TO WRITE YOUR OWN:

1. Dear [name],

2. State your reason for writing this letter.

3. Be honest about any nervousness or apprehension about writing it, and state that you feel it would be a beneficial thing to do.

4. Write down what the main things you wish to express are.

5. Tell the person what you appreciate about them and that you wish them well.

···
···
···
···
···
···
···
···
···
···
···
···
···
···
···
···
···
···
···
···
···
···
··
··
··
··
··
····································

LETTER #20

DEAR INSPIRING PERSON

If there is someone in your life, either a person you know or a celebrity or well-known person who's had an impact on you, whether alive or deceased, write to them and explain how.

WHY WRITE TO AN INSPIRING PERSON?

If someone has inspired you or had an impact, it is a beautiful thing to acknowledge that, recognize the value they have given you, and show gratitude for it.

WHAT TO DO WITH THE LETTER:

This is a letter you may choose to write for your own purpose as an act of gratitude, but you may wish to share it publicly or pass it on to the person if possible.

HOW TO WRITE IT:

Make a list of any people, known to you or not, perhaps people in the public eye or even those you see around your town doing good things, who inspire you. Choose someone to write a letter to and mention all the ways they are an inspiration and how they have had an impact on your life or your attitude.

EXAMPLES:

Dear Princess Diana,

Though you are long gone from this physical world, your memory is not. I am writing to say thank you for being an inspiration in the lives of many, including mine. You had many challenges but faced these all with grace and humility. You knew the importance of being a hands-on mother and giving unlimited love to your children, and you made the most of your media exposure by giving and showing love to others in the world too, especially children. You helped people gain awareness about the impact of land mines and supported the campaign to ban them. You also raised awareness about HIV and helped to dispel myths about how the disease is and isn't contracted. You were in the public eye almost constantly, and you did your best to make sure the focus was put onto other things going on in the world as much as possible.

I admire everything you stood for, and I also admire how, in the midst of everything you went through, you allowed your human nature to shine through and captured the hearts of the world by simply being yourself.

You were one of a kind, and your loss has been hugely felt by so many, but most importantly, what the world gained by your presence was invaluable. Thank you for being who you were and inspiring so many.

From someone who admired you

Dear Woman I Don't Know,

I see you around town sometimes, and occasionally we've smiled at each other as we've passed, but I've never actually stopped to tell you that I think you're an inspiration, so that is what this letter is for.

I see you wrangling your three kids, one in a wheelchair, getting around town and doing things you need to do, and I want you to know you're doing a great job. You might say that anyone in the same situation would do the same, they would do whatever they had to do with what life gave to them, but that doesn't mean you shouldn't be acknowledged. I see how you handle everything with a smile on your face, even when you had trouble reversing your car out of the disabled spot because someone had parked too close to it and you had to get out and check how close it was in order to get back in and try again. You were still smiling, and you just got on with it, like anything was surmountable. I was going to go and help you maneuver, but by the time I got closer you had done it yourself and driven out—much better than I would have done even in my regular car!

I am sure you have moments by yourself when

you cry or feel like giving up, but somehow I know that your strength is so great that you are always able to keep going and looking after your family.

Next time I see you, I think I am going to stop and tell you all this. Or I might just give you this letter.

Thank you for being an inspiration,
A friend you don't yet know you have

BEFORE YOU WRITE YOUR LETTER...

Complete the following sentences:

1. I would like to write a letter to an inspiring person because...

   ....
   ....
   ....

2. After writing this letter, I would like to feel...

   ....
   ....
   ....

3. I will write this letter... (in a journal, on nice paper, etc.)

....
....
....

4. Some ideas on ways to acknowledge, store, or release this letter are...

....
....
....

5. Positive key words that I would like to consider using in this letter
    are...

....
....
....

6. The main ways this person has inspired me are...

....
....
....

TEMPLATE AND GUIDE TO WRITE YOUR OWN:

1. Dear [name],

2. Tell them why you are writing to them.

3. Write down all the ways they are an inspiration and how they have impacted your life.

4. Express any final words you wish to say.

CONCLUSION

Thank you for reading this book and giving the power of secret letters a try! Remember, the power is in the process, and these letters are a helpful way for you to deal with life's challenges and process your emotions. I hope you will continue to use secret letters as an empowering form of journaling at different times in your life and share the benefit of doing so with others.

Remember, if you would like to share any of your secret letters with other secret letter writers or discuss your experiences, follow the link at julietmadison.com for the Secret Letters Project Facebook group, or submit via the website, and your letter may be shared anonymously on your behalf.

To read one last letter from me, please turn the page.

Dear Everyone Involved in the Secret Letters Project,

Thank you for your role, however large or small, in allowing this book to be published, read, and of value to people around the world. Thank you to Joelle Delbourgo, my agent, for believing in this concept and securing and negotiating a publishing deal. Thank you to Anna Michels and everyone at Sourcebooks for accepting this book and investing in it and my career—you are fabulous to work with. Thanks also to my Australian fiction publisher, Escape Publishing, and to Harlequin Australia for permission to include the "Dear Soul Mate" letter from my novel *April's Glow* as an example in this book.

Thanks to the people who submitted the real-life letters, the feedback about letter writing included in this book, and the extra letters to be shared online in support of the book. I loved reading them.

I'd even like to thank those challenges that appeared in my life that prompted my desire to write to express my emotions and thoughts, for without them, I may not have been able to write this book and create a way for others going through challenges to make their journeys easier. I'm grateful for the opportunity to make something positive out of something difficult.

And to my friends, family, readers, booksellers, and fellow writers who support and encourage my career—thank you too.

Love,

Juliet

ABOUT THE AUTHOR

Juliet Madison is an Australian bestselling and award-nominated author of fiction and an inspirational coloring book artist and self-empowerment writer and coach. In the past, she ran a successful business as a naturopath and health coach, empowering people with the tools to manage various health challenges on both a physical and emotional level.

A perpetual student of self-development, Juliet enjoys empowering books and courses that inspire a fulfilling, passionate life and loves writing her own motivational quotes and insightful reflections.

Juliet sometimes got in trouble at school for writing letters to her friends during class and decided to combine her love of writing and her fascination with letters to create a new healing and empowering tool for people to use throughout their lives, as she has done herself.

She can be contacted via her website at julietmadison.com.